Footprints
of a Country Lad

Thomas Alan Coad

Published by
George Mann Publications
Easton, Winchester,
Hampshire SO21 1ES
+44(0)1962 779944

ISBN 9780956087454

George Mann Publications

Contents

~ Dedication ~

My first dedication must be to my dear wife, Gwen. Fifty eight years ago I took her from busy Croydon to quieter rural Hampshire. She has endured the many changes of fortune that marriage to me has entailed with patience and helpfulness through happy times and sad.

To Mary, our dear daughter, I extend much gratitudefor her love, loyalty and support.

Our grandchildren, Kirsty and Danny, have been, and still are a source of joy to us as are our two young great grandsons, Daniel and Jack, also new addition March 2009, Holly Jane.

Finally I must gratefully acknowledge the help of my elder brother, Roy, and his wife Joy. Without their support this small volume would never have been. My other brothers, Harry, and David who is living in New Zealand have also given much very appreciated encouragement.

Foreword

Every life is unique. Each has its own high and low points from which the pattern of an individual's course is woven.

These poems, written at various stages of life, are offered in the hope that others might find pleasure, perhaps also help, in reading them.

My wife and I live in central Hampshire which has been our home for 58 years. We have a daughter, one granddaughter and one grandson and two great-grandsons. Sadly, we lost our son at the age of 19 in a road accident.

Personally, I enjoyed the great benefit of growing up in the country along with three brothers and some of the poems reflect country life. Others portray a Christian faith which was first learned from my missionary parents and later became more vital as a result of life's experiences.

My hope is that folk who read these verses will know the happiness that is found in the simple things of life and the peace that is found in simple faith.

May 2009

Waiting

This poem draws its inspiration from memories of the thirties and forties, whilst waiting for my school bus at the same stop as men who worked at the large railway works at Eastleigh.

I waited at the bus stop as an eager lad of ten,
I waited in the company of cloth-capped working men,
I knew them by their first names, Chas, 'Arry, Ted and Ben.

They talked of building engines and trains that ran by steam,
And wondrous to my young heart did their work world labours
       seem,
Whilst of joining in their efforts would my mind so often dream.

I waited at the bus stop when wailing sirens blew,
As bombers droned their throbbings high up in the summer blue,
And fighter planes with chattering guns shot the bright azure
       through.

Still waiting at the bus stop at the age of seventeen,
With Chas and 'Arry Ben was dead and Ted was a marine,
And sombre war news cast its grey o'er all the English scene.

I never used the bus stop for many a livelong year,
I never built an engine, or cut a deep toothed gear,
My footsteps followed different paths that took me far from here.

Now waiting at the bus stop at the age of seventy two,
Old ladies with their shopping bags and school girls form the
       queue
But Chas and 'Arry, Ted and Ben are waiting with me too.

Eastleigh Dragon

At the Railway Works in Eastleigh, most of the Southern Railway steam engines were built, but many of the expresses did not stop there.

A deep affection dwells in me,
A great nostalgic dream,
That springs from youthful memory
Of the dragon that ran by steam.

On Eastleigh station, stout and firm,
I'd stand on platform two
And feel the trembling flagstones squirm
As the dragon came roaring through.

Express to London, fast it sped,
Shaking the whole town too,
Whilst belching smoke and cinders spread
To hide the other side from view.

But patient could that dragon prove.
When shunting in the yard,
Nudging the waiting trucks to move
With clangs, metallic, loud and hard.

Electric trains and diesel power
Now rule the railway track,
But how I long for just one hour,
To have the old *Lord Nelson* back.

Bishopstoke

The village of Bishopstoke lies a mile east of the town of Eastleigh. It existed long before the town was built in the last decade of the nineteenth century as the result of the railway setting up its large engine and carriage works. Sad to say the white painted railings were changed in colour to a dark shade, thus removing the safety factor for night-time traffic in later years.

Village of rivers and mill race and bridges,
White painted railings by fast flowing streams,
Wide water meads where at even the midges
Swarm in their millions by rushes and reeds.

Gone is that building the water wheel housing,
Where millers once ground the gold Hampshire grain,
Sweet memories linger nostalgia arousing,
Sounds of the waters still constant remain.

Up on the hillside that church's square tower
Marks where the graves of past villagers lie,
For centuries have rested in yon shaded bower,
Whilst summers and winters and waters flow by.

'Eastleigh for Bishopstoke', so read the station
When nothing to look for was there to be seen,
The Borough now dwarfs you, railway's creation,
But older your story, and fairer your scene.

Old Johnny Crow

Thoughts prompted by a sighting on a bright winter's morning.

Old Johnny crow a-top the bare branched chestnut tree,
Sinister and sombre in his cold contumely,
Searching out advantage in the places men don't see;
That lifeless hedgehog lying by the leafless shrubbery.

Now, swooping slow and awesome, he drops upon his prey,
Outspread wings a-casting evil shadows cross the day,
Shadows enhanced by morning sun upon the tarmac way,
As Johnny and his dark mate plunge, their hunger to allay.

Dark birds of gloomy plumage, they forage everywhere,
With cousins rook and magpie they seem to rule the air,
Their lives, remote from ours, yet they have their place, and share
The same breeze and the sunshine that play upon my hair.

Autumn Country Song

Give me a sunny autumn day
With a sharp fresh breeze,
Smell of the lying, round baled hay,
Sway of the half leaved trees.

Warmth of the sunshine beaming through
High white clouds above,
Floating a sky of azure hue.
Coos of a high perched dove.

Nip in the air, that says 'Summer's o'er',
And winters surely due,
But now enjoy the warmth and power,
The sun extends to you.

When chills of northern wind blow strong,
In bitter January,
I'll recall autumn's friendly song,
And pleasant company.

The River Test

The silver Test, fairest of Hampshire's rivers,
Though closely matched by Itchen's sparkling stream.
High upland chalk your crystal flow delivers,
To southward run your waters clear and clean.

Long boating Vikings rowed your course to Wherwell,
And there a battle fought with Saxon men.
A brief but bloody skirmish, so the books tell,
For restless were the days in England then.

Now, through the towns and pleasant village vistas,
Whitchurch and Hurstbourne Priors launch your flow,
By Longparish and Wherwell run your waters,
Chilbolton, Leckford, Longstock, past they go.

At Stockbridge, where the rich and County Gentry,
Their own selective club for fishers hold,
Where Ministers of State and Lords have entry
To dine and talk of angling, I am told.

Houghton and Horsebridge by, your swift currents flow,
Past ancient Mottisfont with Abbey old,
Through Romsey town, where Abbey Church stands mellow,
And Broadlands fair estates your waters hold.

Across low lying wetlands, towards the waiting sea,
Southampton port awaits your constant flow,
Where many a ship waits high tide eagerly,
To cast her moorings and to seaward go.

Grandad's Story

(with Danny aged 3 in 1994)

"Tell me a story Grandad,"
The little boy said
As he lifted his head,
"Tell me a story here now."

So I held him, precious bundle,
Warm and trusting as I sat,
And told him a simple story,
About this, and about that.

Then a joy leapt up inside me,
That echoed days gone by,
Whils't thirty years fell from me,
And another lad was nigh,
A little boy with his sister,
Standing hopefully by.

That too was a simple story,
Told then, forgotten today,
But that moment was gilded with glory,
In a most unforgettable way.

For time with unstoppable motion,
Pursues its untameable race,
But moments of gold are dropped, shining,
To be gathered and held in embrace.

Night-Time Vision

Thoughts after seeing an unexpected vision on arising in the dark hours and looking out of the window.

By night in the misty moonlight
It hung like a billowing cloud,
Motionless in the still nightime,
A flimsy and whispy white shroud.

Simply a Japanese Cherry
Whose glory had gone with the Spring,
By day it was nothing unusual,
A quite unremarkable thing.

When the full moon cast its silver
And foliage threw back the light,
Its trunk was lost in the shadow,
And leaves turned a silvery white.

As a cloud of white vapour it billowed
And hung in the still nightly air,
A vision grace and of beauty
For late-bedding humans to share.

I think of that night-timely beauty
When common sights meet me each day
And ponder that darkness is fruitful
When yielding such radiant display.

All kinds of shadows do meet me
Whilst traversing life's rugged way,
But darkness will bring out the brightness
That cannot be seen in the day.

A Poem to Starlings

The starling is a mobster,
A right gregarious bird,
He always flies in numbers,
A skybound wheeling hoard.

The flock flies with a motion,
That keeps it all as one,
One mind controls their movement,
They wheel in unison.

Two hundred may be perching,
On one large leafless tree,
Yet at a given moment,
Each one flies instantly.

What is the will that leads them?
How do they jointly fly?
Keeping such flawless action,
When hundreds fill the sky.

Some say they're always squabbling,
I don't think that can be,
When wheeling in such numbers,
They take no injury.

How do they know to gather,
In instant noisy meet,
upon my lawn when leatherjacks,
Arrive for them to eat?

I notice that the wagtail,
Delights to tag along,
To join in with the party,
When the starlings throng.

Sleeping Babe

(Mary 1956)

Sleeping babe, for you I pray,
As, born into this world today
In innocence you nestle there
Untouched by any want or care.
Thoughts of the years that lay ahead
Do not disturb your peaceful bed,
For as the moments pass you by
Unheeding you just let them fly.

As beneath your mother's love
Her tender care you daily prove,
This solemn charge to you I give
To keep in trust long as you live,
Treasure up each happy token,
Lay in store each fond word spoken
For as years pass of this I'm sure,
You'll need them, every one, and more.

Sleeping babe, this world is full
Of beauty and of life,
But everywhere the touch of God
Is marred by greed and strife,
So, thankful, note each kind deed done
To imitate the same,
And live your life as unto Him,
Spurn wrong and turn from shame.

Martin

Written in memory of a 19 year old son who lost his life in a tragic road accident after a walk on old earthworks at a hill Just outside Winchester ~ June 1978.

You went out lonely, treasure of our hearts,
Alone you went to the silence of the hill;
The voice that called was strong, too strong to stay from,
For well you loved the peace,the quiet, and the still.

You wandered, happy,on the age old earthwork,
One in your heart with ancient men and ways,
Then looked across the valley and the roadway,
Where the city and its buildings met your gaze.

The city, sunlit hill and valley roadway,
What fateful web this trio were to spread,
Calm hill that lured you, cruel road that slew you,
And city where you'd lie on peaceful bed.

But it was *not* fate that called on that calm evening,
For reasons that we know not, a higher council ruled,
The Lord of Life eternal, with purpose only glorious,
He called, He claimed, He took you, and His way is always good.

A Strong So' Wester

High birds a-wheeling,
Tall birches reeling,
Blown clouds revealing,
Wide patches of blue.

Dry dust a-blowing,
Hoisted flags flowing,
Dead leaf drifts growing,
As wind whistles through.

Tight stringed kites flying,
Hoarse sea birds crying,
Broken plants lying,
A sad sight to view.

From Land's End to Dover,
When high winds are over,
The South will recover,
The stillness it knew.

A Hillside Copse
Viewed and Entered

With azure blue for a background,
A flimsy high network of twigs
Entwined with the silvery branches
An aura of mystery gives.

Before and below the high birches
A mixture of shadings of green
Forms a close cover, alluring,
A tight knit but enticing screen.

At the gateway, one lonely Whitebeam,
Invites one the pathway to tread,
And enter this world of deep mysteries
That lies 'neath the branches o'erhead.

There are giants of Beech, Oak and Chestnut,
And Alders grow nearer the stream,
Besides the Goat Willow and Hawthorn
And some samples more of Whitebeam.

We walk in the woodlands with pleasure,
Delight in the friendship of trees,
And pray that our children's children
Might still enjoy blessings like these.

Resurrection Morning

To the world at large
Was that morning
Different
To any other morning?
When those women
With their spices and ointments
To the graveside came.
Was the early sun's warmth
More chill?
Or did the trees
Droop their branches
And let their leaves drop
In shame?

Were Pharisees
And Sadducees
Abed, content,
Their malice spent?
And did the soldiers sleep?
Had any of them
Once heard the Baptist say
"Do violence to no man"?
And did that man
Who won the cloak
Dare wear it as he walked abroad
On an "off duty" day?

"The deed is done,
What had to be is over,
Finished" we hear them say!
"Time for recrimination gone."
But they are unaware
Of angels rolling off the stone,
Or men in shining clothes
And purposes greater than theirs.
A world of narrow parameters
And plans of short perspective
Bar them in and blind their view
To concepts higher, wider than their own.

Kirsty (aged 2, 1983)

Kirsty is chuckles and bubbles and laughter
Kirsty is gurgling and fun.
Kirsty is dimpled and curly and sunshine
Kirsty's a taste of the sun.

Kirsty comes out with a glad cry to meet one
All bursting to show off her books,
Kirsty knows all the names in the pictures
And how each of her doll's dresses looks.

Kirsty you light up our days and our moments
To bring a bright sunbeam to play
Which cheers up the darkness and brightens the
    shadows
So lighting the passage of day.

Oh Kirsty we are glad that you come to cheer us
We so need your laughter and fun,
For when your young prescence is joyfully near us
We feel the warm rays of the sun.

Conversion

From whence shone that light in the darkness?
From Heaven it only could be,
As, groping my way in the shadows,
It cast its bright beams around me.

As of old to that bigot from Tarsus,
Unexpected and blinding it shone,
Pulling him up in his traces,
The glory of Jesus, God's son.

Oh glory all glory surpassing,
Oh light which brings peace to the soul,
And oh, the sweet love touch of healing,
"'Tis Jesus that maketh thee whole."

Your manger, your cross and your rising,
The path you have trodden for me,
Your death was the price of my blessing,
My pardon was purchased by Thee.

Where is Edenmills?

The railway runs at Edenmills,
Beside the sparkling sea.
On landward side the rolling hills,
Are seen but distantly.

Between the hills and railway track
Lie fields of greens and gold,
Some slightly raised, some dropping back
A village to enfold.

The scene is all of happy calm,
That satisfies the soul.
It basks in sunshine, mildly warm,
And peace pervades the whole.

The sea is on the right as we,
Pursue our railroad run
Its light-glint waves are silvery
Beneath the gleaming sun.

You wonder, where is Edenmills,
Where does this idyll lie?
With peaceful, murmuring brooks and rills,
Beneath a genial sky.

We each must find our Edenmills
Within our inner man,
A place where we meet calms and stills,
Amid life's stress and strain.

For peace springs, not from outward source,
It lies within the heart.
A calming, cooling restful force
That nothing can disrupt.

Why, Why Love?

Why should I love? Love can be hurt,
And love can suffer pain.
Better by far to steel my heart
And never love again.

But love cannot be bidden, "stay",
Controlled to hold or flow,
A crocus will its bloom display
One may not bid it "no".

And love might, wounded, shrink from sight
And withdraw for a while,
But it *must* spring and throw its light,
It's inexorable.

The sacred writer said of love,
That it is kind and strong.
It rises, hope and faith above,
And always suffers long.

Tis only love that can men hold,
With links of *happy* bond,
Bare dutie's calls are hard and cold,
And offer nought beyond.

But love, if let to have its say,
Will flourish everywhere,
It is the only worthwhile way,
None other can compare.

The River Itchen

*The town of Alresford, referred to in verse
two is pronounced as "Alsford" locally.*

At Hampshire's heart, rivulets three,
Meet, to form the primary
Of a river that runs free,
Through lush historic scenery,
Verdant and gently hilled.

The first from eastward sends its flow,
Joined from southward just below
Alresford town's scenario,
From Cheriton, where years ago
Battle's blood was spilled.

To west, a little further on,
A third stream from Northington
Sends the river, fully grown,
To westward move by Ovington,
Its course now amply filled.

Two villages its name then bear,
Itchen Stoke, the first, is near
Itchen Abbas; past this pair,
A village, so named to declare,
A Christian martyr killed.

For Martyr Worthy, one of three,
'Worthy' villages to see,
Turns the river southerly,
Down through Winchester's ancient see,
Where history is revealed.

Twyford and Shawford are the next,
Whom the river runs betwixt,
Here a listener stands transfixed,
By water song and birdsong mixed,
And feels his spirit thrilled.

From Bishopstoke the current strong,
Through the water meads flows long,
Towards its final parting song
At hustling, bustling Southampton,
Whose port is rarely stilled.

Daffodil Time

Golden faces brightly beaming,
Jostling, crowding, waving, teeming,
Undulating, wave like seeming,
Fields of daffodils.

Seen in wide, outspreading masses,
Like a crowd of happy lasses,
Wearing brilliant party dresses,
With bright yellow frills.

Or, seen in somewhat lesser numbers,
'Neath the night owl's daytime slumbers,
Where the fallen branch encumbers,
By the woodland rills.

Always welcome, ever glowing,
Brightness of the Springtime showing,
In many households cheer bestowing,
Upon window cills.

Before the Service

A meditation when quiet in church before the start of the service.

The Bible lies before the cross,
Both raised for all to see.
Its open pages spread across,
That sign of Calvary.

The Bible is the Word of God,
Christ is the living Word.
The written word our daily food,
And He our risen Lord.

The cross on which our saviour died,
On which His blood was spilled,
A symbol, not of hope denied,
But of God's will fulfilled.

The cross points up, Christ glorified,
Its arms all men embrace,
God's Son in heaven now at His side,
On earth, outflowing grace.

Oh help me Lord to take with me,
When going from this place,
An aura of serenity,
A deep and inward peace.

Our Town, Then and Now
1930~2000

About Eastleigh, in Hampshire.
Sad to say that the carrriage works of verse 5 closed in 2006.

It no way was a "country town",
Though set in Hampshire's scene,
A place of industry and toil
Where artisans were seen.

A town of friendly terraced homes,
On streets laid out in squares,
Where honest folk lived honest lives
Without false grace or airs.

Such was the town near which I grew,
Past sixty years a-gone,
A two pence bus ride from my home,
Or threepenny return.

The industries have changed today,
No Loco Works are there,
Where hundreds built steam railroad giants
The ground is hard and bare.

The Carriage Works where coaches for
Rail travellers were born,
Is but a shadow of itself,
But still is working on.

Our Cable Works, where many miles
Of sea-bed links were made,
Is now a site for houses new,
With tarmac pathways laid.

The shopping streets, where friendly stores
Were spread on friendly ways,
Are much the same, though names have changed,
And there are glass-roofed bays.

An indoor shopping mall now stands
In centre of the town,
If winters cold we hold no fear
Of being weather blown.

For truth our town has altered much
Since life cannot stand still,
And all things do change constantly,
They always have and will.

But the old town will still be here,
When we no longer roam
Its streets, but younger hearts will love
It still, and call it home.

God Stood with Us

See Paul's words in 2 Timothy 4.v17

God stood with us,
We could not see
His form with natural sight,
But well we knew
His presence near,
ft buoyed us day and night.

For it is so
For all who learn
To trust His keeping power,
His presence comes
We know not how
And stays with us each hour.

It may perhaps
Fade now and then,
When sorrows voice is strong,
Then with new warmth
We feel again
He's been here all along.

Market Day

The town will come alive today,
For market men are due this way.
Many great bargains they will bring,
Many a luring offering,
Tempting good folk from miles around
To make a journey, hither bound.

Some stalls have canvas tops and sides,
Wide open fronts and smart insides,
Where clothing hangs on rails in rows,
New shirts and skirts and camisoles;
Trousers for hims, and slacks for hers,
Warm overcoats and man made furs.

Here is a gas hamburger grill,
Emitting a strong onion smell,
Whilst next door is a bacon seller
Hard against a fortune teller.
Picture frames and kitchen pieces,
Paper backs, all new releases.

Any article or gadget,
You're sure to find a stall that has it.
Cheap tools from bankrupt dealers' stocks
Wire nails and screws and cupboard locks;
In short, there's everything you need,
And all at lowest price, indeed.

But after five, when all are gone,
When roads are swept and pavements shone,
The local pigeon flock will meet,
After spilled crisps and crumbs to eat,
And folk will pull the shutters down
For sleep to overtake the town.

Fair Oak Fields ~ 1930s-1990s

The village of Fair Oak lies in central Hampshire, 2 miles east of Eastleigh town. During the 1930s. white sand/lime bricks were made there, hence the sand pits mentioned in this poem.

1935

Down through the sloping wild grass,
Toward the copse below,
Dotting the fragrant pasture
Hawthorns and brambles grow.
A verdant hillside clearing
With green sward nibbled low,
Reveals a place where rabbits
For evening frolics go.

Across the copse a wide path
Divides the woods in two.
Running its length a rail track
For iron skips runs through,
Pulled by a patient cart horse
From hand dug sandpits to
A place where hook and hawser
Will uphill each truck tow.

The copse holds mighty elm trees,
Which now stand healthily,
Before the fatal beetle
Works his great savagery.
Great oaks and ash and beeches
Under which hazels lie,
Whose autumn nuts hang sweetly,
For country boys to try.

One wild and windy morning
Three great beeches fell,
They crushed the growth beneath them
And lay across the dell.
But even in their falling
Their branches stood up well,
Providing splendid view points
For climbing boys to scale.

1999

The ever keen bulldozer,
Has ripped the woods away,
Has flattened out the hillside
To stop the rabbits play,
Smart houses, trim and modern,
In gardens now display
The cultivated mutants
Of plants from far away.

You who now live in dwellings
Modern and smartly kept,
I wish you every fortune,
And hold you in respect.
But when I'm looking over
Your gardens, trim and swept,
Remember I am treading,
Where field boys laughed and wept.

Mountain Dreams

The mountain range stands hard and blue,
Against the distant sky.
Its very outline cruel and bleak,
As side by side, and peak by peak,
For height the summits vie.

From miles aback the sweep I view
Where pinnacles point high,
Some lesser knolls look small and weak,
As, set beside the river creek,
They on the fore-plain lie.

The viewing of these distant crests
So full of majesty
Awakens in my wistful heart
Desire to scale each steep rampart,
And learn its mystery.

Yet well I know I never will,
Climb these alluring heights.
But I can trace Nicholas Crane,
Up past where mountain waters drain,
To view far distant sights.

With him may go from Finisterre,
Cross Spanish mountains high.
From French Alps through Helvetia,
To Austria and Slovakia
All mountain pathways by.

Poland, Ukraine, Romania;
All where he trod I'll go,
Bulgaria to Istanbul,
End of his walk remakable,
Through rains, sunshine and snow.

I thank him much for letting me,
Through pages eloquent,
To join him on his journings,
To share with him so many things
And places that he went.

Wilhemina's Birthday

Out of the town house window,
As we were walking by,
Came sounds of childish laughter
And happiness filled the sky.

"Happy birthday to you, Wilhelmina,
Happy birthday today to you,
Our party's for you, Wilhelmina,
The whole day belongs to you too."

My whole hearts with you, Wilhelmina,
Best wishes to you and your friends,
For many more days, Wilhelmina,
My goodwill to you now extends.

I don't know your face, Wilhelmina,
Your height, nor the shade of your hair,
I probably never will see you,
But may all your life days be fair.

Riverside Walk

Through the meadow, slowly streaming,
Reflecting greens and blue,
Under trees with boughs o'er hanging,
Which cloudless sun shines through.
Silent, save for gentle lapping
And woodpecker's tree bark tapping.

Calmly, peacefully and placid
Do run the waters here.
Slow depths, dark, mystical, furtive,
Unruffled till the weir
Brings a loud, tumultuous splashing,
Sends the waters downward dashing.

Many moods and many changes,
On your long course you see,
Often flowing mildly, gently,
Then fast and aimfully.
Ever onward, never staying,
From your channel never straying.

Your constant stream speaks re-assurance,
To my mind's changing frame,
That, whilst my lot is brief and passing,
Your's will remain the same,
When later generations see you,
Walk as I now gladly with you.

Remember the 'Bevin Boys'

In-the lean and hungry thirties, as schoolboys we were told,
That coal mined from deep workings was our nation's black
      toned gold,
This dark and dusty mineral, brought out by sweating men,
Was the life blood of our country, the fuel on which it ran.

All the people's railways, great ships that plied our trade,
Power stations, gas works, and all things that were made
In vast and noisy factories, all hospitals and schools,
Wherever workmen laboured, or tradesmen wielded tools,
Every hearth in every home, all farmsteads large or small,
Every aspect of our lives was energised by coal.

Then rose a mighty conflict as nations met in war,
Young men in many thousands went to many a distant share.
They fought their country's battles, by air, at sea, on land,
In clouds, on waves, in jungles, mountains and desert sand.

From home the factories fed them with equipment for the fray,
As coal grew short for want of men they found another way,
Young men from farms and offices, from shops and schools
      were made
To go and work with miners, to learn their sweatful trade.
They faced not death at awful scenes which came in violent bout
But worked with men who lived with death, each day, year in,
      year out.

Youngsters from country outdoor life, who'd never been
      enclosed,
Young men with tender hands and knees, who'd always been
      disposed
To think of future days in banks, or a director's chair,
Musicians, sportsmen, all were sent, darkness and sweat to
      share.

Some worked the rattling rail tracks, a mile or more below,
They trudged through dark low tunnels, heads and shoulders
      bended low.
They crawled down long coal faces, through burrows two feet
      high,
They lugged the rams head drills with heavy cables coiling by,
They shovelled coal on rubber belts with knees both raw and
      sore,
Where two men worked to clear a stint of twenty yards or more.

Long years have passed, and many now know nought of
      'Bevin Boys',
The mining men with whom they worked, are 'not required'
      these days,
But young men died in deep coal pits as well as on the field
Remember them, they gave their all; their duty too fulfilled.

To an Aged Pastor

A quiet peace,
From many years,
Of walking with his Lord.
The knowledge of
"His" service done,
A sole and full reward.

He sought no place
Of high renown,
Nor to be widely known.
But faithfully
He preached the word,
And cared for all his own

All that he said
All counsels given,
Were wise, considered, plain.
All those who heard
Knew every word
Was caring, sound and sane.

His great support
Through all the years,
And helpmeet in all strain.
His loyal wife
Who worked with him
And shared his every pain.

They share with joy
The memories,
Of many happy hours.
Sad times of grief,
Then sweet relief,
Throughout long serving years.

Your strength in age,
Contented minds,
Speak far more fluently,
Than many sermons
Ever could
Though spoken lucidly.

Eternity,
Burns in your eyes
And motivates your love,
That many years
Of deeds and words
And kindly actions prove.

A Penitent's Prayer

After reading Psalm 51

You did not cast me, Lord , away
Though I so badly failed.
I grieved you sore, you suffered long,
And yet your love prevailed.

The pain I left in other hearts,
I know will linger long.
The hurts I cannot mollify,
Or counteract the wrong.

The debt I owe all who forgave,
My debt oh Lord to you,
Humbles my heart, gives me resolve;
To broken vows renew.

Nevermore, from this day on,
Dare I refuse to show
Forgiving grace to anyone
Who may beseech me so.

From Calvary's deep pain and woe,
The prayer of Christ my Lord,
"Father forgive, they do not know,
The nature of their deed".

As He forgives, His grace to me,
Binds me for evermore,
With ties of joyful loyalty,
That ever will endure.

My Gwen

I met Gwen, my dear wife of well over 50 years, whilst we were both on holiday in North Wales in 1947. She was from Croydon and we married in 1950, after which we lived in Hampshire in the Eastleigh area.

What colour was your hair?
Mousey you called it!
What an unapt name
For those soft light brown strands
That fell about your lovely face
And to your shoulders came.

There must be fitter,
Worthier words to use
But I can think of none:
For e'en the best of names
Could not descibe
The allure of that tone.
I well remember though
How it glinted fair
In that north Wales sun.

Now Hampshire sun, for fifty years,
Has bleached those locks so fair,
Though Surrey first shone, down upon
The ringlets of your hair.
And wartime years in Sussex
Lent their own tonal share.
But silver white,
They now shine bright,
And never past have shone so fair.

St. John:
After Reading His Gospel

These pages, written long ago
Speak with such power today,
For living truth, with living force,
Your ancient words portray.

You tell of three short wondrous years
Spent with a man from whom
The very word of God was heard,
His light and life for men,

You heard the spoken words of life,
You saw His healing might,
You knew Him as the Son of God,
Source of that life and light.

The very world was made through Him
In which as man He trod,
But yet the race that owed Him life
Refused His living word.

Your eyes beheld His deep resolve
To do the Father's will,
And even on a cross to die
That purpose to fulfill.

You saw His grace expressed to all,
To all men only good,
You heard Him tell how He would die
Before the nails and blood.

You stood with ten bewildered men
Who saw His risen form,
You spoke with Him, and ate with Him
Who'd left the fast sealed tomb.

So sure you were, so free of doubt,
That half a century more,
You lived with hardships, savage threats,
His gospel to declare.

Old age brought you no respite,
But strong, you hate endured,
In bonds at four times twenty years
For service to your Lord.

You wrote that others might believe,
And find life in their faith,
Believing in your living Lord
Who triumphed over death.

Gladly I take your words to heart,
And gladly own Him Lord.
In grateful trust I place my hope
In Christ, the living Word.

Drift Lane

Drift lane meanders down the hill
Under rustling leaves and boughs.
A minute flow, hardly a stream,
Beside the roadway tinkling goes,
Through grassy meadows leading down,
To where the racing river flows.

By pastures sweet and living green
High hedges grow on either side.
Far overhead the high clouds float
And in the growth coy field mice hide,
Whilst blackbirds nest above their heads
Shielded below the harrier's glide.

This shaded country way is not
A frequent route for active men,
As busy lives have not the bent
For reverieing in the lane,
And, seeking much, in seeking lose
The gladness that they here could gain.

Oh sad the thought that some could miss
In lives too full of frantic chase,
An opportunic chance of bliss
Or a momental glimpse of peace
Through deviating from the way
And pausing for an hour's release.

Kind happy way, contented scene,
Long may this lane meander still,
And may the tinkling brook remain
All to run steady, down the hill,
Unruffled by the furious chase,
That never ends, and never will.

In the Abbey Gardens at Winchester

Here, seated on my parkside bench
This placid August day,
A scene of happiness and peace
I joyfully survey.

Behind; a gently running brook
Moves with a murmuring sound,
Whilst sounds of childhood pleasure flow
From swings and slides beyond.

Before; an area of green,
Perhaps two acres wide,
Has cared for grass, round flower beds,
Each colourful and bright.

Large marigolds of orange hue,
Bordered with blue and gold,
Asters and dhalias neatly placed,
A pleasure to behold.

Upon the lawn young mothers meet,
Squatting the green grassed ground,
Whilst, safe and happy, toddlers play
By pushchairs parked around.

The red brick house beside the gate,
Partly four centuries old,
Has Georgian frontage to the park
Pleasingly neat and bold.

It's fit that in this ancient place,
Where Romans lived and played,
And Saxon kids enjoyed their sport,
Still happy play is made.

Wild Meadow Land

Behind, before, and acres wide,
Knee high the grasses grow,
Gently they sway in gentle breeze,
Small rustling sounds the eardrums please,
Whilst, multi-hued, wild flower heads show
Dotted across the wide meadow.

No plough or scythe or farm machine,
For generations past,
Has touched these fields, no horse or cow,
Has pastured been, no scrounging sow
To forage has beenlet loose here,
No sheep and no far ranging deer.

Some smaller mammals scamp about,
Low nesting birds find peace.
High flying kites soar overhead,
Night owls with silent wings outspread,
As dusk and darkness bring their prey
Scampering through the grassy way.

In nearby woods the badgers dwell,
And foxes have their dens.
Shy rabbits burrow underground,
Hunter and hunted, both around,
But as I cross this peaceful field
Only its calmness is unveiled.

We need such areas as this,
Where natural creatures thrive;
For wild life, for plants and trees
Small mammals, insects, humming bees,
To freely live out Nature's plan
And dwell in harmony with man.

Across the spreading countryside
We leave our prints around.
We sow our crops and harvest grain
We cultivate with might and main,
But wild zones must be left to stand
Or much will vanish from our land.

Sounds of Rural Engalnd

With restful quiet spread around,
When first I sit I hear no sound.
This clement summer afternoon
To rest and muse is opportune,
Only the grasses in the breeze
With rustling sounds my senses please.

But when upon my back I lie
Gazing upwards dreamily,
Some other resonances drift
And fall upon my ears to lift
Me from my reverieing state
And other things to contemplate.

From four fields off there floats a sound
As combines work the wheat around,
And with a distant gentle purr
A highway's never stayed murmur,
Whilst nearer, fainter, buzzings flow
From insects humming as they go.

These sounds, all part of countryside
Drop on my semi-concious mind
And cause ones fancy to reflect
That parts of life all intersect.
A driving city gent is heard
As background to the song of bird.

But little notice does he take
Of all the living things that make
The total sum of life within,
The region through which he can spin,
Of all the unseen busy days
And ups and downs of rural ways.

September Sunset

Widely outspreading, right to left,
And high above unfurled,
This golden glory covers all
To brightly tinge the world.

A crimson tint the clouds display,
Mixed with their flaxen gold.
No royal canopy could show
Such splendour when unrolled.

Late evening sees a shining disc
Behind the hills descend,
Whilst darkness creeps across the sky
Spelling the daytime's end.

Majestic was the huge display
Of glory, spreading wide;
And awesome is the darkening sky
Of fading eventide.

But sweet the evening call to rest
As silver rays point high
Signalling night-time's swift onset
While waning sun shafts die.

Approaching Storm

Sombre, approaching from the west,
Doleful and darkly threatening,
A thick cloud brooding, high outspread,
Wide, charcoal grey and menacing,
Glows brightly silver at its verge
As covered sunshine overhead
Catches the stern black storm clouds edge.

A stillness hushes all below
So recently by breezes blown,
Whilst chillness be-numbs man and beast
At Nature's fury bearing down.
As darkness overtakes the scene
In houses lights begin to shine;
I turn the key and enter mine.

Welcome my refuge, as the crash
Of thunder clap rattles the sash,
And wind and rain arrive to dash
Their bouncing shafts of water down.
Swift rivulets spring up to run
And quickly grow to flood the drain
And overwhelm the culvert main.

This awesome show, of Nature's might,
Turning the summer day to night,
Brings trade and commerce to a halt
And provokes reason to reflect
On powers beyond the charge of men,
On forces great beyond our ken
That take no heed of where or when.

The fury lasts but half an hour,
As natural wrath abates its power,
Wild winds have blown much foliage down
And scattered things about the town.
All water in the flowing drains
Runs out to musical refrains
As town its normal life regains.

Life's Pathway

No preparations could be made
For taking to this road,
Unsought the highway has been laid
Which needful must be trod.

I know not why or whence I came,
What lies before, beside;
Who sent me on, where lies my home?
I need, I need a guide.

So many voices to me call
Claiming to point the way,
Whil'st different loves and feelings pull
To hold and cause delay.

Various signs a clue provide,
Where oft divides the track.
Which should I take? I need a guide
Lest I should wander back.

I need a guide who knows the way
From having passed before;
Has walked these valleys night and day
And crossed each open moor.

Midst seeking help and finding none,
A muted voice I hear,
No outward form to gaze upon,
But definite and clear.

I know that voice as one which spoke
To men in Galilee,
"Take on you my untaxing yoke
And follow after me."

I've walked the path you follow now,
I know the journey's end,
There is no danger or no foe
Which I did not contend.

The door to life I opened wide
Through death upon a tree;
Through ressurrection death defied,
For men to follow me.

For travellers now I wait ahead,
But also by each side,
I walk with every aching tread
Ever the goal and guide.

Age and Youth

One pleasant autumn afternoon,
A brightly sunny day,
An old man took a parkland walk
And watched the youngsters play.
As he stood on the sideline
A young lad spoke to say,
"Tell me please what you have seen
In times so far away."

"In my life," the old man said,
"I have seen so much.
Things that you will never see,
Touched things you'll never touch.
Fields of standing sheaves of corn,
High built ricks of hay,
Steam rollers, traction engines
On a traffic free highway!"

"In this life things always change,
For nothing ever will
Remain the same from year to year,
Life never will stand still.
But much your eyes will see my boy
As your life winds its way,
Wonders of which I've never dreamed
You will see in your day!"

"In this life all have their share
Of years to live, and deeds to dare,
But changes will come everywhere.
My father lived with older ways
That changed before I knew,
But those who came before him lived
Their transformations through,
So hanker not for things now past,
The future is for you."

The Village Fair ~ 1935

This really is a day of joys
For village girls and village boys.
A fair has set up in the field
That Farmer Gray had left untilled,
For seven days it there will stay
To bring delight and gaiety.

The roundabouts have been unpacked,
By swings and shies, green canvas backed,
And bumper cars are set to run
With shrieks and cries of village fun,
The helter skelter, down to shoot,
With many a whoop and many a hoot.

All lads and girls will make their way
With bobs and tanners to outlay,
The village youth will come as one,
With even the policeman's son.
This week is special every year
And brings such happiness and cheer.

Across the village floats the sound
Of music loud, and laughs abound
As happy folk, both old and young
From near and far mingle among,
The stalls and sideshows spread around
This fallow plot of unused ground.

The friendliness of such events,
Gave to our village life a sense
Of unity and pride of place.
Together everyone had space
To live their life, and yet to feel
Part of a common bond of weal.

November Sighting

Three chestnut trees, bold, side by side,
Before the bright November sky,
All leaves are shed, yet still a hint
Of green imbues each meshed outline
Which arches widely, reaching high.

A branching dome, a twiggy dome,
Each standing giant here is set,
Whilst rays of autumn sun reflect
From light clouds wandering overhead,
And glitters through each silhouette.

Below and strewn upon the grass
Are spikey, half decayed nut shells,
The fruit, by squirrel long purloined
With hazels, for the winter stored
Under the boughs in which he dwells..

With native oaks, as sentinels,
These great arborial titans stand,
Regretful of their comrade elms
Which once stood with them in the fields
And forests of our motherland.

Jobsworth Bob the Blackbird

Each day we lay out upon our lawn bread for the birds. Our usual customers are about 20 sparrows, some pied wagtails, a robin, a couple of mistle thrushes and the inevitable crows and pigeons, collared doves too. However there is always one male blackird waiting under the forsythia when the bread is spread. He considers it to be his duty to keep all other birds off. Out he runs at the sparrows who simply flutter up only to land behind him and carry on. He will "deal with" other small birds, chase off his own kind and cousin thrushes and even eye out the pigeons and crows.

He stands in awesome sole command
A self-appointed guard,
Though far more fare than he could need
Is spread upon the sward.

His "jobsworth" hat has been mislaid,
But still his task to foil
And hinder any other bird
From sharing in the spoil.

He rushes from his hiding post
Each sparrow to repel,
Bright yellow beak with point outstretched
To other birds expel.

All fellow members of his tribe
Thrushes and redwings too,
Are scuttled off with equal zeal,
He eyes the pigeons through.

Little success his efforts yield
For as the small birds sail
Before his charging wild foray
They pitch behind his tail.

Oh self-appointed lookout I
Know all your kind too well
You crop up in so many a guise,
At many a place you dwell.

How sad the lot you self impose
Upon yourself each day,
For here you stay and never move
Whilst others fly and play.

A Hampshire Lad

Although born in London, within sound of Bow bells indeed, I was brought to Hampshire by my parents before the age of two and therefore by every memory I am a Hampshire man. There are family roots with Cornwall and a sense of "Cornishness" persists within one's heart, but from all recollections and friendships I am a Hampshire man and my wife a Surrey girl.

Not Hampshire born, but Hampshire bred
I called myself a Hampshire lad.
Grew up midst Hampshire fields and trees
'Twas Hampshire nettles stung my knees,
And Hampshire air stirred up the breeze.

I knew a Hampshire village school,
Where three strict ladies held their rule,
Daily we all would well be fed
On homegrown veggies from the shed
And crusty Hampshire village bread.

The country life of England then
Produced strong independant men
Who loved their lot and loved their place
And did not yearn to more embrace
But lived content within their space.

In Hampshire's borders may be seen
From west to east a changing scene.
Old forest land and open heath
Gives way to hills, grasslands beneath,
With hearty crop producing earth.

Northwards our counties stage reveals
Pasture land and grazing hills,
With sheep and cattle in their herds
By arable, productive fields
And higher open treeless wolds.

Counties of England each embrace
Their own prospects of scene and place,
And each has sons and daughters who
Are to their bounds and friendships true
Loving the land their fathers knew.

Bright November Morning

Though bright, a hazy mist enclothes
The low November sun.
A chill, not sharp, but livening
Bites lightly on the skin.

The southward sun throws shadows long
As shining through thin mist,
It every clump and every stone
Picks out upon the grass.

One's blood flows warm and eagerly
Through veins and arteries,
And folk speak brightly, cheerily,
Buoyed by the gentle breeze.

Cold winter's bite is not yet felt,
Though summer's heat has gone,
So these are days for active life
And purposeful action.

Each month has its own recompense,
November's special ploy,
Is when the late autumnal sun
Lifts up the heart with joy.

Betula Pendula

Not far from where we live is a small area of grass. Upon this green are a number of trees, and about 25 yards apart stand a silver birch and a weeping willow. The first is tall, stately, slim and graceful; in another setting she would really be a "lady of the forest". The second is thickset, bent over and humble in form especially after loosing one of its main boughs in a storm, abject and pleading although graced with luscious green down hanging foliage.

"*Betula Pendula,*" how grandly she bears
The pride of her family name.
With arrogant, off handed gesture she waves
Her graceful slim leaf bedecked frame.

She feigns not to notice the mendicant form
Beseechingly bowed at her feet;
Though truly she well knows deep down in her heart
She is much pleased to see him entreat.

It gratifies greatly her narcistic mind
To think he adores her so well;
She will not say yes and she will not say no,
She will keep him bowed down at her will.

Salix Chrysocama his family name,
A thickset and submissive crew;
How could he presume to implore for her hand –
Such pairing, it never would do.

Oh tell him to go and forget such desires,
Release him from pangs of his pain.
Don't keep him so long, so bowed down and so low
But let him find freedom again.

Grandad's Flowers

Whilst planting out daffodil bulbs I suddenly called to mind a long forg0tten incident from childhood. A lady from outside the village had recently come to live in a cottage up the lane. This lady told my mother how a bright crop of daffodils had bloomed in her front garden. One day she saw a young girl standing by her gate, gazing at the blooms. A little crossly she asked the child why she was staring so, to be shaken by the youngster's reply: "Those daffs, my grandad planted them there, for me."

"My grandad planted those for me,"
The little maid said wistfully.
"He dug the soil and turned the ground
As I was skipping all around,
And said when he had raked it through
These daffs I'm planting here for you."

I think he knew he would be gone
Before their springtime faces shone;
He cried when grandmother was dead,
He didn't think I saw – I did:
"When you see these," he said to me,
"Think of your grandmother, and me."

I do not think he ever thought
His cottage would be sold and bought,
He'd lived here all his life you see.
My Mum grew up with brothers three
And moved a little down the road
When I was born, with me and dad.

"I hope you will not mind if I
Come to your gateway frequently
At springtime when the fresh daffs grow
To brightly let their faces show,
So that I, for some moments few,
Can think of him and grandma too."

Rainbow Surprise

So full of marvel and surprise
A small boy awestruck stood.
Reflected in his wondering eyes
The bow, so high, so bright, so wide
Hugely outspread o'er copse and mead
Shining, brilliant, multi-hued.

Its background dark, paynes grey the cloud
Which recently the torrents bore,
But boldly, gleaming, wide and proud
This radiant arc shines more and more
As sun reflects and prisms glow
Kaleidoscopic – heaven's bow.

Well may you marvel little man
When first you see this glorious sight,
For mystery and wonder can
Enfold the mind with pure delight.
You ponder on the scene you see,
It also grasps and dumbfounds me.

A Tip for Harassed Mothers

'Moo-cow' biscuits are the ones
To give your daughters and your sons,
They will not ever make a mess
Upon a shirt or on a dress
And they are guaranteed to quell
The sulky whimper or the yell.

If Jane or Jack should start to quibble
You can encourage them to nibble
By telling them to leave the head
And bite the tail end instead,
So by the time the head is eaten
Their tantrums will be truly beaten.

It really is amazing how
A biscuit blazoned with a cow
Can work such calming soothing wonders
To quieten young passions thunders,
And so make sure you've always got
Some laid by in a jar or pot.

Always when you out with kiddies
And would be ready for their paddies,
Carry in your bag a packet
Or place some biscuits in your jacket,
This way you will well prepare
For any toddlers temper flare.

The Pied Wagtail

From all the birds that deign to grace
Their presence on my garden space
My heart holds out a special place
For one smart dapper little ace.

He's neatly turned in white and black
With slender etchings down his back
And has the happy perky knack
Of standing out amongst the pack.

He bobs his tail rather than wags
With bold, defiant, carefree jags,
He never waits and never lags,
His stretched out tail he never sags.

Where other birds may hop or flutter
He runs along the empty gutter,
To perch upon that pile of clutter
Beneath the sun house open shutter.

It seems he likes to land among
The crowding starlings when they throng
Upon the lawn, he joins along
Those swarming birds of grating song.

But in the usual run of play
He is his own bird day by day
And follows his determined way
To fly or run where're he may.

I'm glad he does not fly afar
When seasons change and cold winds jar,
He cheers my heart when grey skies mar
The winter scene both near and far.